THE KEYS

to the

KINGDOM

by Lacey Whittaker &
Rita Krone

Edited by Lil Barcaski

Published by: GWN Publishing

www.GWNPublishing.com

Cover Design: Kristina Conatser Captured by KC Design

ISBN: 979-8-9859746-9-0

Dedication

This is for anyone out there searching, maybe lost and who needs a key to get them through a minute, day, trial or a lifetime.

ABOUT THE
Book

Are you looking for simple keys to get through life? Do you yearn to get to the heart of the matter quickly, not wanting to waste any time being stuck? In this book you will find keys to help unlock questions you may not have the answers to.

Why does Jesus want to give us keys?

I believe it is to survive in this world. The world chokes out the simple way He intended us to live with the busyness of life. When we live here, it's hard to see clear. It's hard not to be blinded by evil. He gives us keys to endure and overcome and walk like He has called us to walk here on earth.

A KEY TO
Forgiveness

Forgiveness unlocks peace. Forgiveness is truth. It holds you accountable and makes you choose. Will you live with offense and hate, or will you choose to forgive in more than one way? How many times will you forgive? Will it be 100 x 10?

I will choose no matter how long it takes. I will choose forgiveness no matter how hard it is to face. I will choose forgiveness in the end because when I choose, I am the one who wins. It takes time. It takes heart. Be kind, gentle, and loving. Love the unlovable. Keep repeating this until you feel compassion and a release.

A KEY FOR
Speaking in Tongues

It's a powerful prayer, intercession with our great helper, the Holy Spirit that knows exactly what we need.

A KEY TO
Peace

Going straight to Jesus. Letting go. Being in His presence. Living there. Being in Gods will. Pleasing God.

A KEY TO
Saying Yes

Blessing upon blessing, be an open vessel to be in the will of God. Be His hands and feet. Know not knowing what you are fully saying yes to but trust Him in your yes.

> *"The Living One! I was dead, but now look—I am alive forever and ever. And I hold the keys that unlock death and the unseen world."*
>
> —REVELATION 1:18 TPT

A KEY FOR
the Orphans

Love them. Care for them. Welcome them. Hear them. Trust God has them. He is the most loving Father.

A KEY TO
Choose Life Over Death

Be reborn. Live like Jesus. Forgive. Choose life.

A KEY FOR
the Widows

Pray for them. Help them. Love them. Care for them.

A KEY FOR
Respect

Know God loves everyone. Pray for everyone. Everyone is on their own journey. Bless them. Have a true heart for everyone. Respect God and respect your neighbor as yourself. Respect yourself by loving yourself.

A KEY TO
Being Rebuilt

Thanking Him. Praising Him. Letting go. Holding on to what He has given you instead of the loss. It's a new day. Be refreshed. Be encouraged. Smile. Dream.

A KEY FOR
Success

Going straight to Jesus. Asking His will
His way. It's the high road of praise. It's the
I don't think it's supposed to look this way.
It's heaven's way we walk and see. It's light
and how He has made us to be.

A KEY FOR
Overcoming the Past

I look at where I was and see where I am now. I try to keep doing better each day. Never straying back to my old ways. Living a brand-new way. A new path I take. This encourages me to keep walking the narrow way. One way. One step forward. I may stop but never will I walk back.

A KEY FOR
Visions

For me, He uses puzzle pieces. He showed me two puzzle pieces at the beginning of my journey with Him. One was Him; one was me. He then connected them. The next puzzle was a bigger puzzle. It was my life with Jesus and each yes was a puzzle piece which is added and put together with each act of obedience He has called on my life in this season. I see this vision now from where I started. It's a little over half completed. These visions can help me see from where I have started and keep me going, encouraging me to move forward with each yes. Each season the puzzle will be completed, and I will start new with the next.

"I will give you the keys of heaven's kingdom realm to forbid on earth that which is forbidden in heaven, and to release on earth that which is released in heaven."

—MATTHEW 16:19 TPT

A KEY TO
Being Thankful

Take time out each day. Set aside 10 minutes and thank Him. If you don't know what to thank Him for, just say thank you. The more I thanked Him, the more I found to be thankful for. It also jump-started the next step in my journey walking with Jesus.

A KEY TO
Receiving Gifts

Look to the Heavenly Father knowing full well He wants to bless us and take care of us with both earthly and spiritual gifts. Acknowledging Him and thanking Him for every gift He gives. Receive with open hands.

A KEY TO
Overcome Worry

Telling Jesus out loud even though He knows your worries. Say them to Him. Let Him have every worry. Then repent of your worry. If you don't give them to Him fully, He can't take care of them. Sit with Jesus and tell Him as you would a friend.

A KEY FOR
Compassion

I believe the key is seeing Jesus on the cross. The cross He bore. Compassion sums up Him on the cross that day. He was beaten, spit on, mocked and left to die. Many rejected Him. He looked up to heaven and said, Father, forgive them for they do not know what that they are doing." That's true compassion. We should all strive to have compassion as Jesus did that day. We can have compassion because He did, and He tells us to do so. Go have compassion today on all those enemies that have persecuted you. See how compassion really frees you.

A KEY TO
Compassion When Hurting

The more compassion you have for someone, the bigger protection you have around yourself. It frees you. To be free is to be at peace in everything.

A KEY TO
Overcoming Hurt

I would first say, what are you holding onto? Is it your pride? Is it something deeper, maybe an insecurity you have been carrying? Hurt hurts but letting go, forgiving, choosing to live unoffendable, knowing we all are human, and all have faults. Loving, forgiving, hurt and knowing your worth in Christ. Your worth is your fight. Spirits may rise and come against but, Jesus wins. Forgive, repent and love again. That hurt will fade away and you will see another day.

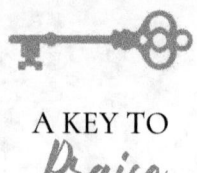

A KEY TO
Praise

Be thankful. To know He is Lord of Lords, King of Kings. Worship. Be grateful. No matter what we are going through, He has us.

A KEY TO
Help Release

Crying. It's okay to cry. It's okay to feel. Let go. Cry out to Jesus.

A KEY TO
Handle Grief

Don't blame or shame yourself. Give it to Jesus. Know they are in the loving arms of Jesus. That's our hope. Letting them go. Know the Lord has plans for you to continue here. Go through and don't get stuck in your grieving. Call on Jesus. He hears your every cry. Be thankful to Jesus for loving them and know His plan is always the best plan even though we may never understand. He sees the whole picture. We may only see in a tunnel at the time of overwhelming grief.

A KEY FOR
Friendship

Listen to each other. Be there. Show up. Don't control. Be led by the Holy Spirit. Respect. Have compassion. Thank God for them. Love them for who they are and how they encourage you. Spend quality time with them. Pray for them. Do not judge them but give them the hard truth.

A KEY ON
Raising Children

First, give them up to the Lord. Teach them about Jesus. Show them. Lead by example. Let them make mistakes. Pray for their growth and relationship with Jesus early on. Have the hard talks. Listen to them. They have a lot to say. Respect their childlike faith. They have lots to show and teach you too. Encourage them. Love them, and let them prosper in their calling and purpose.

A KEY FOR A
Godly Marriage

Respect. Love them for them. Do not control. Be led by the Holy Spirit. Love each other. Serve one another as Christ has called us to serve. Let go of the petty. Pick your battles. Pray for one another. When one is weak, the other one be strong and willing to help. Listen to each other. Communicate well.

A KEY FOR
Health

Stop the worry and stress. Stop the small, constant worries that you keep going over and over and over in your mind. Slow down the thoughts, make them obey. Release stress. Take deep, deep breaths. Smile. Let go of control. Walk in peace. Release, release, release.

A KEY FOR
a Healthy Soul

Run to the lover of your soul. Do what you love. Feel what you feel. Go be free in nature and all He has created for us to enjoy. Find a quiet place. Sit and soak. Let go. Feel His presence around you. Slow down, rest and simplify. That's how He has called us to enjoy this life.

A KEY TO
Letting Go

Forgiveness first. Have compassion on the person who hurt you. Not all see the way you may see. Jesus took the hurt and pain. He knows and sees what we go through, and He hurts for you too.

A KEY TO THE
Heart of Jesus

To be like Jesus. To walk as He walked. Love like He loved. See the way He sees. To say yes as He said yes to God. To serve as He served. To sit and be still as He sat and went away to pray and be alone with His Father.

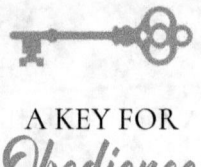

A KEY FOR
Obedience

I believe the key for obedience is to Meditate on His word. Listen to Him speak to you through the Holy Spirit. Obey and follow what He says. He will lead and He will guide but you will have to surrender your pride to live in full obedience. Live in the vine. Bear much fruit. This is how I chose to obey and walk with You, Lord.

"Take hold of my instructions; don't let them go. Guard them, for they are the key to life."

—PROVERBS 4:13 NLT

A KEY TO
Joy

Joy, oh joy, is that deep feeling in your soul. It's the joy that never leaves but always flows no matter what. Joy is within. No matter what, joy always wins. His strength is our joy, and when we depend on Him, joy always shouts, it always wins. Rejoice and be glad.

A KEY TO
Love

The key to love is to be loved and love others. Love like our Father always loves. Forgive yourself and be fine. Love true. Love died so we could live. Never let the enemy take this love from you. Love, love, love is a powerful thing. Go spread it everywhere and watch it reign.

A KEY TO
Happiness

Happiness comes with letting go of control. Living in union with our Father. Trusting Him with everything. Happiness comes when we fully know that He, our loving creator, is in control.

A KEY TO
Freedom

To die to self. Live for Him. Be free and win. Die to self. Kill the flesh. Kill it. Kill it. Kill the flesh. Live with Him. Trust Him. Let go. Be free. That's the key.

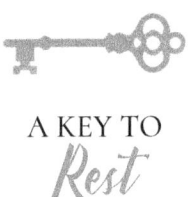

A KEY TO
Rest

Be still and know.

ABOUT THE
Authors

A pair that lived as aunt and niece for many years, one day longed for something more and took a journey going deeper to find a void they were missing. It was Jesus. Now their hearts are both hoping to see everyone learn to have that one relationship they couldn't live without; teaching others to hear Him for themselves. They both are a part of True Love Ministries in Bourbon, Mo. They love to sit, hear, and write, and be in the house of prayer together.

www.ingramcontent.com/pod-product-compliance
Lightning Source LLC
Chambersburg PA
CBHW070453130626
46553CB00006B/2388